Success With

Contemporary Cursive

SCHOLASTIC

Editor: Ourania Papacharalambous
Cover design by Tannaz Fassihi; cover illustration by Kevin Zimmer
Interior design by Mina Chen
Interior illustrations by James Loram

ISBN 978-1-338-79833-3
Scholastic Inc., 557 Broadway, New York, NY 10012
Copyright © 2022 Scholastic Inc.
All rights reserved. Printed in the U.S.A.
First printing, January 2022
1 2 3 4 5 6 7 8 9 10   40   29 28 27 26 25 24 23 22

INTRODUCTION

Parents and teachers alike will find *Scholastic Success With Contemporary Cursive* to be a valuable teaching tool. Students will enjoy the humorous art as they learn and practice contemporary cursive handwriting. Step-by-step letter formation will help students master all 26 upper- and lowercase letters of the alphabet. Students will also practice writing words, sentences, numbers, and short paragraphs. The stationery on page 48 can be used for a variety of teacher-directed activities. Teaching these valuable handwriting skills to eager learners will be a rewarding experience. Remember to praise the students for their efforts and successes!

TABLE OF CONTENTS

$\mathcal{A}\,a$

Use your best handwriting to copy the letters, words, and sentence below.

a a *a aaa*

a a *a aa*

a a *a aa aa*

Atlantic *Atlantic*

ape *ape*   apple *apple*

Active ape awakens

angelic alligator.

angelic alligator.

B b

Use your best handwriting to copy the letters, words, and sentence below.

B B B B B

b b b b b

B b B B B b

Baltimore Baltimore

baby boy boy boy

Beautiful baboons blow

bubbles in a bathtub.

B

$\mathcal{Cc}$

Use your best handwriting to copy the letters, words, and sentence below.

$\mathcal{C}$ $\mathcal{C}$

$\mathcal{c}$ $\mathcal{c}$

$\mathcal{Cc}$

Cincinnati

candy   *case*

Confident camels carry

cute, cuddly cats.

Dd

Use your best handwriting to copy the letters, words, and sentence below.

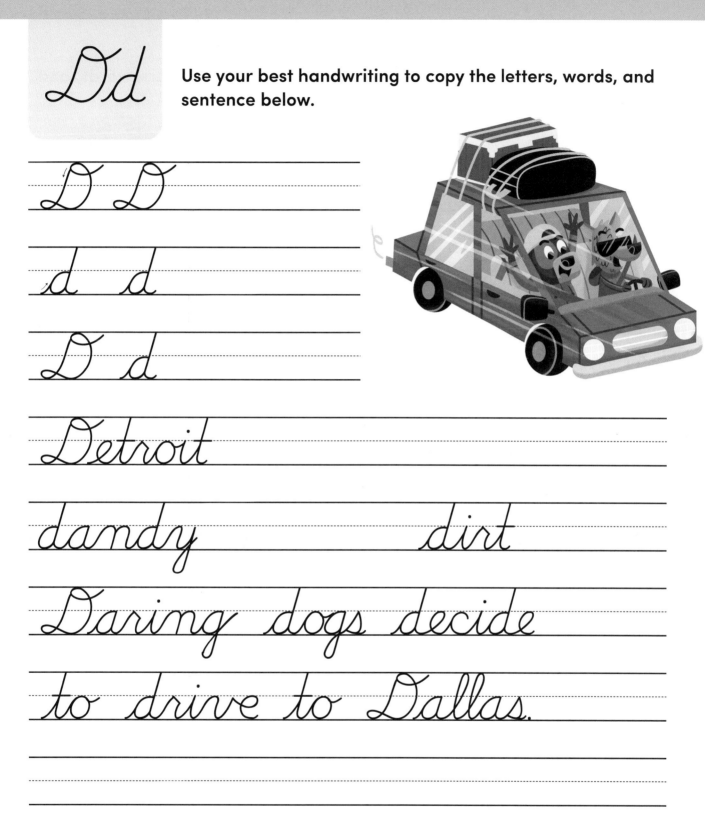

D D

d d

D d

Detroit

dandy   dirt

Daring dogs decide

to drive to Dallas.

Ee

Use your best handwriting to copy the letters, words, and sentence below.

E E

e e

E e

Erie

ever   eye

Elegant, elderly elephants

eagerly eat eggs.

Ff

Use your best handwriting to copy the letters, words, and sentence below.

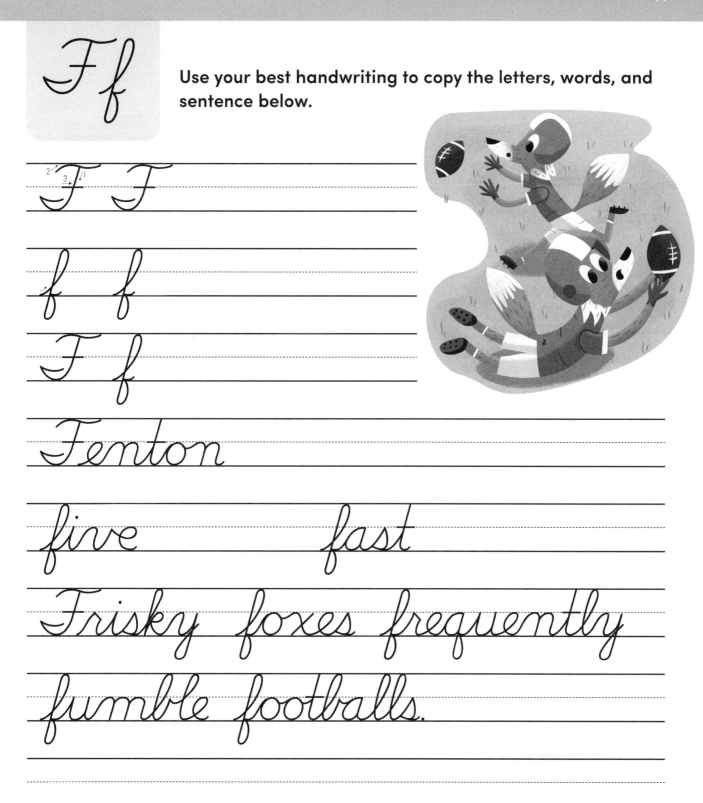

F F

f f

F f

Fenton

five   fast

Frisky foxes frequently

fumble footballs.

Gg

Use your best handwriting to copy the letters, words, and sentence below.

HEHEHE...

G G

g g

G g

Green Bay

gauge   grate

Giggling geese gobble

giant green gumballs.

Hh

Use your best handwriting to copy the letters, words, and sentence below.

H H

h h

H h

Hanover

honor   halt

Happy hamsters have

huge, hilarious hats.

$\mathcal{I}i$

Use your best handwriting to copy the letters, words, and sentence below.

$\mathcal{I}$ $\mathcal{I}$

i i

$\mathcal{I}$ i

Inglewood

ink   ill

Idle inchworms ignore

irate insects in Iowa.

$\mathcal{J}j$

Use your best handwriting to copy the letters, words, and sentence below.

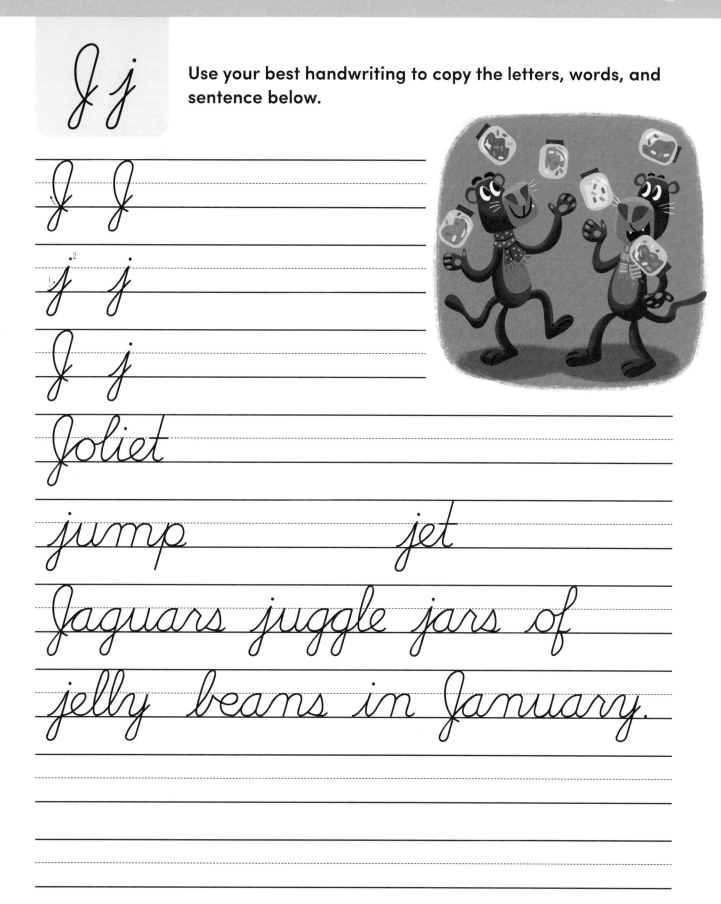

$\mathcal{J}$ $\mathcal{J}$

j j

$\mathcal{J}$ j

$\mathcal{J}oliet$

$jump$ jet

$\mathcal{J}aguars$ $juggle$ $jars$ of

$jelly$ $beans$ in $\mathcal{J}anuary.$

K k

Use your best handwriting to copy the letters, words, and sentence below.

K K

k k

K k

Kenosha

kite   kick

Kind kangaroos knit

socks for kids.

Ll

Use your best handwriting to copy the letters, words, and sentence below.

L L

l l

L l

Littleton

lock   little

Lazy lobsters leisurely

lounge on lawn chairs.

M m

Use your best handwriting to copy the letters, words, and sentence below.

M M

m m

M m

Missoula

miss   movie

Many merry mice

make mushy meatballs.

n m

Use your best handwriting to copy the letters, words, and sentence below.

n n

m m

n m

Newton

navy   next

Nine nocturnal newts

nightly navigate north.

Oo

Use your best handwriting to copy the letters, words, and sentence below.

O O

o o

O o

Omaha

over   oboe

Odorous otters order

olive oil over oysters.

P p

Use your best handwriting to copy the letters, words, and sentence below.

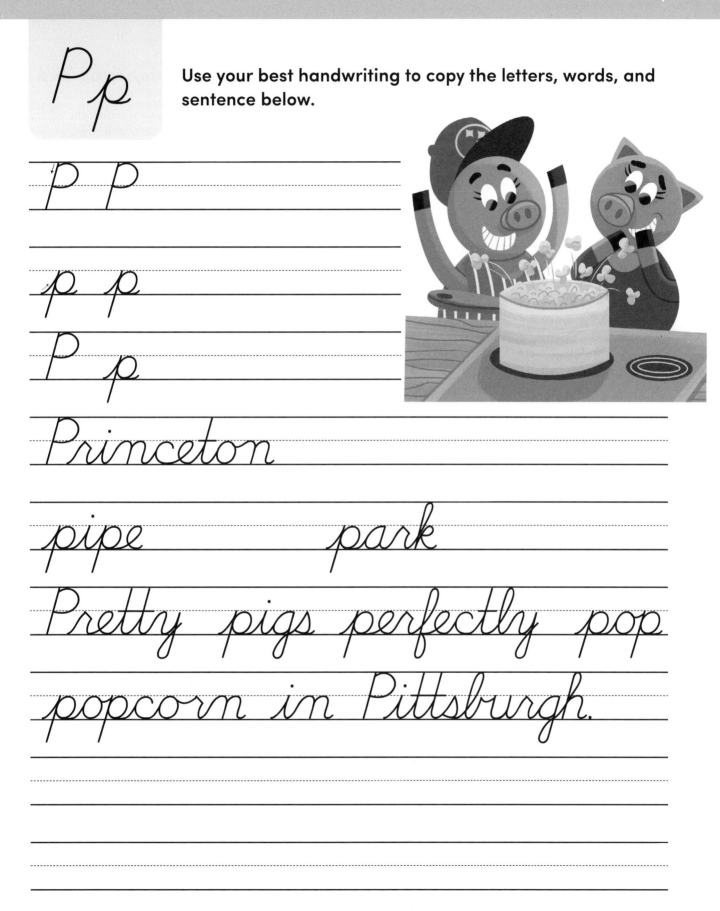

P P

p p

P p

Princeton

pipe   park

Pretty pigs perfectly pop

popcorn in Pittsburgh.

$\mathcal{Q}q$

Use your best handwriting to copy the letters, words, and sentence below.

$\mathcal{Q}$ $\mathcal{Q}$

q q

$\mathcal{Q}$ q

Quincy

quick   quit

Quaint queens quickly

and quietly quilt.

R r

Use your best handwriting to copy the letters, words, and sentence below.

R R

r r

R r

Rochester

rich   rear

Restless reindeer rapidly

run races.

$\mathcal{S}s$

Use your best handwriting to copy the letters, words, and sentence below.

$\mathcal{S}$ $\mathcal{S}$

s s

$\mathcal{S}s$

SKUNK SOAP

SKUNK SOAP

Seattle

sense safe

Sleepy spiders sell

smelly skunk soap.

Tt

Use your best handwriting to copy the letters, words, and sentence below.

T T T

t t t

T t

Texarkana

total   tea

Talented, toothy toads

teach talkative turtles.

$\mathcal{U}u$

Use your best handwriting to copy the letters, words, and sentence below.

$\mathcal{U}$ $\mathcal{U}$

u u

$\mathcal{U}$ u

Urbana

utter   use

Uniformed umpires

usher upset unicorns.

$\mathcal{V}\,v$

Use your best handwriting to copy the letters, words, and sentence below.

$\mathcal{V}$ $\mathcal{V}$

v v

$\mathcal{V}\,v$

Vancouver

vivid   *vat*

Vain vultures

vigorously vacuum.

Ww

Use your best handwriting to copy the letters, words, and sentence below.

W W

w w

W w

Westover

women   will

Wiggly worms wander

westward with whistles.

Xx

Use your best handwriting to copy the letters, words, and sentence below.

X X

x x

X x

Xenia

axis   exit

Xavier Ox x-rayed

six extra xylophones.

Y y

Use your best handwriting to copy the letters, words, and sentence below.

Y Y

y y

Y y

Yorktown

yacht   yet

Youthful yaks yell.

"Yeah, yellow yo-yos!"

Z Z

Use your best handwriting to copy the letters, words, and sentence below.

ZIMBABWE

Z Z

Z Z

Z Z

Zanesville

zipper   *zero*

Zany zebras zestfully

zigzag to Zimbabwe.

A–Z

A B C D E F G
H I J K L M
N O P 2 R S T
U V W X Y Z

Write.

_____

- -

_____

- -

_____

- -

_____

- -

_____

a–z

a b c d e f g

h i j k l m

n o p q r s t

u v w x y z

Write.

_____
- -
_____
_____
- -
_____
_____
- -
_____
_____
- -
_____

Numbers 0–9

Use your best handwriting to copy the numbers below.

0 0

1 1

2 2

3 3

4 4

5 5

6 6

7 7

8 8

9 9

© Scholastic Inc.

Our Solar System

The sun is the center of our solar system. It is the only star in our solar system. The planets and their moons all orbit the sun. The sun provides heat and light to the planets and their moons.

Write.

_____

_____

_____

_____

_____

_____

_____

_____

_____

_____

_____

Ancient Astronomers

People who study the sun, moon, planets, and stars are called astronomers. Cave people were some of the first astronomers. They drew the different shapes of the moon on the walls of their caves. Long ago, sailors studied the stars to help them travel. The ancient Greeks studied many of the planets.

Write.

© Scholastic Inc.

What Is a Year?

A year is the time it takes for a planet to orbit the sun. A year on Earth is 365 days. It only takes Mercury 88 days to make a trip around the sun. However, it takes Uranus 84 Earth years and Neptune 165 Earth years to orbit the sun one time.

Write.

From Hot to Cold

Some planets are so hot or so cold that people cannot live on them. Some days, it is 800°F on Mercury. On Venus, the temperature is nearly 900°F! The temperature on Uranus and Neptune is about -370°F. Earth's highest recorded temperature is 134°F and the lowest is -128°F.

Write.

How Many Moons?

In our solar system, scientists have found over 200 moons. Saturn has 82 known moons. Jupiter has 53 known moons, and Earth has only one. New moons are being discovered all the time.

Write.

Speedy Mercury

Mercury is the planet that is closest to the sun. It spins slowly, but it moves around the sun very quickly. Mercury was named after the speedy Roman messenger for the gods.

Write.

Beautiful Venus

Venus is the easiest planet to see in the sky because it is the closest to Earth. It is sometimes called the Evening Star. The Romans named Venus after their goddess of love and beauty. Venus is so hot, it could melt lead. It has an orange sky.

Write.

Our Incredible Earth

Earth is the only planet known to have life. It is the right distance from the sun to give it the perfect temperature to have water in all three forms—liquid, vapor, and ice. Although 70 percent of Earth's surface is water, its name means "soil."

Write.

Mysterious Mars

Has there ever been life on Mars? That remains a mystery. Scientists are studying the possibility of past, present, or future life there. Mars is often called the Red Planet because the rocks on its surface look like rust. Mars was named after the Roman god of war.

Write.

Sensational Saturn

Saturn is the second-largest planet in our solar system. It is most famous for its seven rings made of glittering pieces of ice. Saturn was named after the Roman god of agriculture.

Write.

_____

_____

_____

_____

_____

_____

_____

_____

_____

_____

_____

_____

_____

King Jupiter

Jupiter is the largest planet.
It is so big that 1,300 Earths could
fit inside of it! That is why the
Romans named it after the king
of the Roman gods. Jupiter spins
faster than all the other planets.

Write.

Understanding Uranus

How can anyone understand very much about a planet nearly two billion miles away? Uranus was the first planet to be discovered through a telescope. It was named after the Greek god of the sky.

Write.

_____

_____

_____

_____

_____

_____

_____

_____

_____

_____

_____

_____

_____

Not Much About Neptune

Neptune is difficult to see even
if you have a telescope. It is nearly
three billion miles from the sun. Neptune
takes 165 Earth years to orbit the sun
once. Neptune was named after the
Roman god of the sea.

Write.

What's Up With Pluto?

Scientists used to think that Pluto was a planet. Now we know it is too small to be a planet. It is a dwarf planet. Pluto is far away from the sun—about 3,670,000,000 miles!

Write.

_____

_____

_____

_____

_____

_____

_____

_____

_____

_____

_____

_____

_____

_____

_____

_____

Flying Rocks

Between Mars and Jupiter are chunks of rock that circle the sun. There are thousands and thousands of these flying rocks called asteroids. Asteroids come in many shapes and sizes. Some even look like potatoes!

Write.